A GUIDE TO CORALS FOR THE MINI-REEF AQUARIUM

BY DR. HERBERT R. AXELROD

Graphic Design by Sandra Taylor Gale

Published by T. F. H. PUBLICATIONS, INC.,
1 TFH Plaza, Neptune City, N.J. 07753
Completely manufactured in Neptune City, NJ by TFH.

This book is based upon the larger textbook A Guide to the Selection, Care and Breeding of Corals for the Mini-Reef Aquarium **also written by Dr. Axelrod. This is merely a quick guide for the identification and care of corals in the mini-reef aquarium.**

AVAILABLE AT YOUR LOCAL PET SHOP.

Distributed in the UNITED STATES to the Pet Trade by T.F.H. Publications, Inc., One T.F.H. Plaza, Neptune City, NJ 07753; distributed in the UNITED STATES to the Bookstore and Library Trade by National Book Network, Inc. 4720 Boston Way, Lanham MD 20706; in CANADA to the Pet Trade by H & L Pet Supplies Inc., 27 Kingston Crescent, Kitchener, Ontario N2B 2T6; Rolf C. Hagen Inc., 3225 Sartelon St. Laurent-Montreal Quebec H4R 1E8; in CANADA to the Book Trade by Vanwell Publishing Ltd., 1 Northrup Crescent, St. Catharines, Ontario L2M 6P5 ; in ENGLAND by T.F.H. Publications, PO Box 15, Waterlooville PO7 6BQ; in AUSTRALIA AND THE SOUTH PACIFIC by T.F.H. (Australia), Pty. Ltd., Box 149, Brookvale 2100 N.S.W., Australia; in NEW ZEALAND by Brooklands Aquarium Ltd. 5 McGiven Drive, New Plymouth, RD1 New Zealand; in Japan by T.F.H. Publications, Japan—Jiro Tsuda, 10-12-3 Ohjidai, Sakura, Chiba 285, Japan; in SOUTH AFRICA by Lopis (Pty) Ltd., P.O. Box 39127, Booysens, 2016, Johannesburg, South Africa. Published by T.F.H. Publications, Inc.

MANUFACTURED IN THE
UNITED STATES OF AMERICA
BY T.F.H. PUBLICATIONS, INC.

CONTENTS

INTRODUCTION

With the advent of proper filtration, lighting and water movement there are very few obstacles to the care and maintenance of corals in the mini-reef aquarium. The selection of this equipment depends upon the size of your mini-reef tank (the larger, the better!), the availability of the proper equipment from your local aquarium supplier, and the depth of your knowledge on the subject of living corals.

PROPER LIGHTING

The proper light depends upon the species you wish to keep. Those species of coral which contain zooxanthellae (symbiotic algae) require varying amounts of moderate to strong light. MODERATE lighting is obtained from the usual hood filled with normal fluorescent tubes made especially for reef aquaria. HEAVY lighting requires VHO fluorescents, or anything which is super-strong but still fluorescent. METAL HALIDE LIGHTING is the strongest of lighting and is highly recommended since you can adjust the power and direction of the light by simply moving it. This, of course, can't usually be done with fluorescents. Metal halide are hot and must be kept comfortably away from the mini-reef tank (perhaps 18 inches or more). Work with your local aquarium supplier. If your local supplier cannot or will not assist you, find one who will. You NEVER want to buy supplies or live stock (including corals) from dealers who aren't experts in their fields. You must rely on the dealers to supply you with the equipment that you need to be successful. He also must be able to guarantee the health of all living things you buy from him.

Pet shops carry lamps in both standard output and VHO (very high output) to insure that your corals receive the quantity and quality of light they need to survive. Photo courtesy of Energy Savers.

PROPER WATER MOVEMENTS

The whole idea behind a mini-reef aquarium is to imitate a living reef. All reefs are subject to water movements caused either by tides or waves, or usually both. You have to imitate that water movement

Artificial sea salts are widely available in a number of different formulations. Photo courtesy of Coralife/Energy Savers.

in your mini-reef aquarium. Trying to imitate waves isn't very simple. I use a dump bucket. This is a small container set on the edge of the tank. It is slightly off balance so when it fills with water it tips into the aquarium. As far as I know this equipment is not sold, so maybe you can make your own or live without it.

Water movement is necessary for many reasons. Waste products, debris, sloughing off of 'skin' and settling parasites can only be moved through the movement of water. Trace elements and oxygenated water can only be brought to the corals by water movements. Many corals can sense water movement and some retract their polyps if there is too much or too little water movement.

CAPTION TAGS

Each caption for a species has a background color. This indicates the degree of difficulty the author has experienced with these corals. You might have a much different experience. The author sent these evaluations to several experts ...THEY could not agree, in which case the author's evaluation was maintained. You will probably have a slightly different experience. The captions tags will, at least, be a guide as to what to expect.

BEGINNER

INTERMEDIATE

ADVANCED

Green background tags indicate corals which are recommended for beginners without any serious experience. Yellow backgrounds indicate hobbyists who have success in maintaining a normal marine aquarium and who want to try corals. The red background is for thoroughly experienced hobbyists only. They have perfect marine tanks and are successful with other marine invertebrates as well as some of the other coral animals.

Water movements can be compared to flags flying in the breeze. Maybe you can even put a flag of sorts in your aquarium to measure water flow. In any case, think of a flag violently waving. That's the maximum amount of water movement for your mini-reef. Few corals want this vigorous water movement. If the flag almost stays fully extended, that would be HEAVY water movement. At half mast, it would be MODERATE water movement. Anything less is SLOW or LITTLE water movement and it is only recommended to remove toxins from the vicinity of the coral.

HOW THIS BOOK IS ORGANIZED

It doesn't make much sense to organize this book according to scientific families or groups which the average hobbyist will not be able to understand. Instead we have adopted the system which now exists in the marine fish trade. This system is based upon what the coral looks like to the imaginative eye! Thus we'll have brain corals, moon corals, disk corals, elephant skin corals, velvet corals and even soft corals.

If you want a more scientific book read Dr. Elizabeth M. Wood's book **CORALS OF THE WORLD.**

IMPORTANT NOTICE

Very few coral specimens exist in the same color, shape and size wherever they are found. Color variations are the most obvious differences. Thus some corals are often mis-identified. The photos in this book are intended to help you recognize a coral's scientific identity. It is the only book which features corals in their natural range for without this information, identification is difficult if not impossible. Corals are identified by the characteristics which are often impossible to see in the living animal. You must be able to examine their skeletons.

Once you have enough experience, you will be able to observe a situation and know to move this piece closer or further from the light, or to give that coral more water movement.

Learning is what experience is all about. One year of serious coral-keeping will make you a successful mini-reef hobbyist.

BROWN OR GREY CLOSED BRAIN CORAL, ***Favia matthaii,*** is excellent for beginning mini-reefers. Light or heavy lighting, modest water movement and slow growth. Photo by Walt Deas .

BRAIN CORALS

The term *brain corals* is merely an expression of what people think looks like a brain. Corals have no brains! They do not think or have reason...they merely react to external stimuli and rely upon genetic codes to guide their growth and reproductive ritual.

1. 

2. 

3. 

Many pet shops break down their so-called **brain corals** into categories called **moon corals** and **pineapple corals.** Essentially, brain corals which have uniform, circular or roundish crater marks, are called 'moon corals.' Moon corals which are tan (the color of pineapples) are called 'pineapple corals.'

These are all corals with large polyps and hard skeletons. None are very difficult to maintain in your mini-reef aquarium, but they do need maximum fluorescent lighting.

1. *Favia pallida*
2. *Platygra lamellina*
3. *Favites abdita*

FLAT RED BRAIN, LOBO, ROOT, OPEN BRAIN CORAL, *Lobophyllia* species.

There are many *Lobophyllia* varieties which have not as yet been identified scientifically. This species appears from time to time from the Maldive Islands. It thrives on low water movement, high lighting with 8-10 hours of intense fluorescent lighting daily and weekly feedings of newly hatched brine shrimp when their tentacles are extended at night.

FLAT GREEN BRAIN, *Lobophyllia corymbosa*,

Forskål, 1775.

Prefers little water movement but substantial lighting of full fluorescents 8-12 hours per day. May be fed newly hatched brine shrimp in the evening when their tentacles are exposed. Though not aggressive, they should be planted with lots of growing space. This is a common coral found from East Africa to the Red Sea to Australia and Tahiti.

FLAT BRAIN, ROOT, TOOTH, LOBO, OPEN BRAIN CORAL, *Lobophyllia hemprichii*,

Ehrenberg, 1834.

A very common coral which requires low water movement and heavy lighting.They often acclimate to lower lighting, but 8 hours of full fluorescent lighting is standard for this very common species. May be fed weekly with newly hatched brine shrimp when tentacles are extended at night. They are not fast growing but should be isolated from direct contact with neighbors.

DENTED PURPLE BRAIN, *Symphyllia radians*,

Edwards & Haime, 1849.

This is a very prevalent species in the Maldive Islands where I found them on EVERY reef I investigated. They did well in my mini-reef aquarium. They need 10 hours of strong light, very little water movement and weekly feedings of newly hatched brine shrimp in the evening when their tentacles are bared. They occur in many colors, but the purple variety seems to be available most of the time.

DENTED BROWN BRAIN, *Symphyllia recta*,

Dana, 1846.

A common species of the Maldive Islands, this species is also found in grey, green and red but for some reason only the brown is exported. It requires very modest water motion, 10 hours of intense fluorescent lighting and occasional feedings (weekly) with freshly hatched brine shrimp when the tentacles are extended, usually at night. Colonies are brain shaped (rounded).

GROOVED BRAIN, *Oulophyllia crispa*,

Lamarck, 1816.

This is the typical brain coral mode; the adjacent photo shows the coral expanding in an aggressive manner because there is nothing to impede its growth. The same is true in the mini-reef aquarium. If you want a lot of corals, plant them close together and watch them attack their more docile neighbors. Peace is achieved with plenty of living room...a common requirement for most living things.

GREEN BRAIN CORAL, ***Blastomussa merleti,*** is not difficult to maintain in the mini-reef. It needs moderate to heavy lighting, moderate water movement and is slow growing (an advantage).

RED BRAIN CORAL, *Blastomussa wellsi,* is not difficult to maintain with moderate lighting and water movement. It is non-aggressive in the mini-reef aquarium. Photo by Dr. Gerald R. Allen & Roger Steene; computer enhancement by Jan Balon

BROWN CLOSED BRAIN OR PINEAPPLE CORAL, ***Platygyra daedelea,*** requires moderately heavy light, moderate water movement and is slightly aggressive which means it should have some room from its coral neighbors. Photos by Walt Deas.

GREEN OPEN BRAIN CORAL, ***Trachyphyllia geoffroyi,*** is for mini-reefers with a little experience, though many beginners acclimate them without any apparent difficulty. They require medium lighting, moderate water movement and they grow slowly as do all brain corals. Photo by Walt Deas.

GREEN OPEN BRAIN CORAL ***Trachyphyllia geoffroyi,*** grows isolated and is easily collected for the mini-reef. Photo by Walt Deas.

BROWN PINE-APPLE CORAL, ***Platygyra lamellina,*** is suitable for the mini-reefer with a large tank of 50 gallons or more. It has moderate lighting requirements, moderate water movement needs and is not too aggressive. Photos by Walt Deas, Dr. Gerald R. allen and Roger Steene.

GREEN MOON CORAL, ***Favites abdita,*** is excellent for beginners. It requires low to heavy lighting, moderate water movement and is slow growing. Photo by Walt Deas.

PINEAPPLE CORAL, ***Favites flexuosa,*** is excellent for the beginner. It requires from light to heavy lighting, moderate water movement and is slow growing. Photo by Walt Deas.

BOULDER OR BRAIN CORAL, ***Montastrea magnistellata,*** is ideal for the beginning mini-reefer. Lighting is acceptable at low to high levels; moderate water movement and lack of aggressive growth makes this the ideal candidate as a first coral. Photo by Walt Deas.

True-Leaf, Anchor & Grape Corals

This group of corals has many aliases. When dealers can't readily identify a coral they give it their own descriptive name. Thus, in this group of corals with large polyps and reef-building calcium carbonate skeletons, we can find corals with such common names as *true-leaf, anchor, grape, hammerhead, frogspawn, torch, pom-pon, etc.* They all are easily maintained and recommended for beginners. They require substantial VHO (very high output) fluorescent lighting, and slow to moderately moving water. Many of them have stinging tentacles. Handle them only with gloves. These stinging tentacles are also used against neighboring corals, so keep them isolated as they are aggressive.

1.

2.

3.

This group of corals generally spawns by casting eggs and sperm into the water randomly, hoping the two elements will meet and new corals will begin to grow.

1. Euphyllia ancora
2. Euphyllia glabrescens
3. Euphyllia cristata

FROGSPAWN CORAL, *Euphyllia divisa*, is named after the typical mass of frog's eggs which symbolizes the radiant tips of the polyps. The polyps are divided by the extended calices. Easily managed with moderate to heavy lighting, moderate water movement and lots of room between itself and its neighboring corals. Photo by Walt Deas.

ANCHOR CORAL, *Euphyllia ancora*, is very easy to maintain providing trace elements are replaced regularly. This means a 25% water change every few weeks. They need moderate to heavy lighting and normal water movement via a canister filter. They are very aggressive as they extend exploratory polyp fingers. Photos by Dr. Gerald R. Allen, Roger Steene and Dr. Elizabeth M. Wood.

TORCH CORAL, POM - PON CORAL, GRAPE CORAL *Euphyllia glabrescens*. Requires modest to heavy lighting, slowly moving water and no neighbors as this is an aggressive species. Photo by Dr. Gerald R. Allen & Roger Steene.

***Euphyllia* species,** Requires modest to heavy lighting, slowly moving water and no neighbors as this is an aggressive species.

GRAPE OR FROG-SPAWN CORAL, *Euphyllia cristata*, is slightly more difficult to maintain than the other known *Euphyllia* species but if you have kept others then try this one, too. It needs a moderate water current, 8 hours of strong light per day and cannot tolerate touching another coral. Photo by U. Erich Friese.

TORCH CORAL, *Euphyllia glabrescens*, requires moderate to heavy lighting, moderately moving water and separation from other coral animals. Photo by Walt Deas.

BUBBLE CORAL, ***Plerogyra sinuosa,*** is a beautiful and very easy coral for beginners. It requires moderate lighting, moderate water motion and lots of space between it and the next coral animal. Photos by Walt Deas.

PEARL CORAL, ***Physogyra lichtensteini,*** requires moderate lighting and water motion, and plenty of growing room as it kills neighboring coral animals. Photos by Dr. Elizabeth M. Wood.

MOON CORAL, ***Galaxea astreata,*** requires some skill and experience and is not recommended for beginners. It needs substantial lighting, moderate water motion and extensive separation from its neighbors. Photo by Walt Deas.

MOON CORAL, ***Galaxea astreata,*** clearly showing the coralites. Photos by Walt Deas.

GALAXY CORAL, ***Galaxea fascicularis,*** is for the advanced mini-reefer. It needs a lot of light (10 hours of 4-tube light per day in a 50 gallon tank), moderate water movement and space so its tentacles cannot reach its neighbors. Photo by Walt Deas.

THE GREEN STAR CORAL, ***Galaxea* species,** is extremely difficult to maintain in the average mini-reef aquarium. It requires moderate to heavy light, moderate water motion and lots of room. It probably needs a rare trace element for they live for a few months and then die. Photo by Walt Deas.

GREEN DISK, *Fungia scutaria*, needs 9 hours of intense light and moderate water movement. It is dangerous to other corals in which it has contact. Photo by Walt Deas.

***FUNGIA* SPECIES** require 8-10 hours of strong light per day, moderate water movement and space between it and its coral neighbors. They are the most difficult corals that are recommended for the beginning mini-reefer. This photo shows a group of developing *Fungia*. Photo by U. Walt Deas.

MUSHROOM OR FUNGUS CORAL, *Fungia fungites*, requires 8 hours of good light per day, moderate water movement and separation from other corals. Photo by Walt Deas.

PURPLE MUSHROOM CORAL, *Fungia danai*, requires strong lighting 8 hours per day, moderate water movement and separation from neighboring corals. Photos by Walt Deas.

FUNGIA SCRUPOSA requires the same care as *Fungia danai*, but is more sensitive to trace element shortages. Photo by Walt Deas.

***Heliofungia actiniformis*,** the Long-tentacled Plate Coral, requires moderate lighting, a moderate water flow and separation from its neighbors. Photo by Walt Deas.

Heliofungia actiniformis has long polyps and tentacles, perhaps the longest of any coral. Photo by Walt Deas.

NEPTUNE'S CAP CORAL, ***Halomitra pileus,*** has moderate lighting needs, moderate water flow and is not aggressive against other corals. Photo by Dr. Elizabeth M. Wood.

ELEGANCE CORAL, ***Catalaphyllia jardinei,*** is a beautiful coral for beginners. It can take moderate lighting, a light water movement and is not too aggressive. It is ideal for the beginning mini-reefer. Photo by Dr. Herbert R. Axelrod.

GOLDEN ELEGANCE CORAL, ***Catalaphyllia plictata,*** is a wonderful coral for beginners. It requires the same care as *C. jardinei.* Photo by Prof. C.W.Emmens.

Catalaphyllia **species** looks and acts like a sea anemone. This attracts anemonefishes as you can see in this wonderful photo. This is a very easy species to care for with moderate lighting, water movement and space. Photo by Gerhard Marcuse.

GREEN ELEGANCE, ***Catalaphyllia plictata,*** is suitable for beginning mini-reefers. It requires moderate lighting and water motion. It needs space between itself and its neighbors. Photo by MP&C Piednoir Aqua Press.

Caulastrea tumida is not a typical species of the genus *Caulastrea,* but it does wonderfully well in the aquarium with moderate lighting and a modest flow of water. It does not bother other corals. A great species for beginners! Photo by U. Erich Friese.

TRUMPET CORAL, *Caulastrea echinulata,* is easy to care for with moderate light and water movement. It is not aggressive either. Photo by Dr. Elizabeth M. Wood.

THE CANDYCANE, *Caulastrea furcata,* can only be positively identified by its skeleton, as shown here. It requires moderate water, moderate lighting and is not aggressive. Photo by Dr. Elizabeth M. Wood.

ELEPHANT NOSE, ***Mycedium elephantotus,*** requires moderate lighting, moderate water flow and is not aggressive, but it is not for beginning mini-reefers. Photo by Walt Deas.

ELEPHANT SKIN OR SEA CACTUS, ***Pachyseris speciosa,*** requires a substantial water flow and a lot of light. It is not aggressive. Photo by Walt Deas.

Pachyseris rugosa is rare and expensive. It is fairly difficult to maintain but it has the same requirements as *P. speciosa.* Photo by Walt Deas.

BUTTON CORAL, ***Cynarina lacrymalis,*** has modest lighting requirements, modest water motion and is not aggressive. This beauty is nice for the more ambitious beginning mini-reefer. Photo by Walt Deas.

Cynarina lacrymalis occurs in many colors. Photo by Walt Deas.

BROWN DOUGHNUT, ***Scolymia vitiense,*** may also be red or even green. It has modest lighting needs, moderate water movement and is not overly aggressive. Photo by Dr. Patrick Colin.

PURPLE DOUGHNUT, ***Scolymia lacera,*** was photographed in Jamaica. It is the easiest of the *Scolymia* to maintain and require moderate water movement, moderate lighting and is non-aggressive. Photo by Dr. Elizabeth M. Wood.

DOUGHNUT, ARTICHOKE OR AUSTRALIAN SAUCER CORAL, ***Scolymia australis,*** is a mini-reef favorite which appeals to hobbyists ready to graduate to a slightly more difficult flower animal. It has modest lighting needs, moderate water movement and is not too aggressive. Photo by U. Erich Friese.

YELLOW CUP CORAL, ***Turbinaria frondens,*** requires moderate lighting and slightly lower temperatures about 78 °F. Moderate water movement and growing room are required for this fast-growing species. Photos by Walt Deas.

CUP CORAL, *Turbinaria peltata*, presents small problems which are easily solved with moderate lighting and water motion and room to grow as they are fast growers but do not attack neighbors. Photos by Walt Deas.

PAGODA OR CUP CORAL, *Turbinaria mesenterina*, requires moderate water motion and lighting. It requires growing space. Photo by U.Erich Friese.

YELLOW SCROLL CORAL, *Turbinaria reniformis*, requires moderate water motion, moderate lighting and space to grow. Photo by U. Erich Friese.

PIZZA PIE, *Turbinaria* species, is a relatively easily kept species which requires moderate water movement, moderate lighting and is not aggressive. Photo by U. Erich Friese.

PIMPLE CUP SPOTTED CORAL, *Turbinaria stellulata*, is the easiest of the genus to maintain in your mini-reef aquarium. It requires the usual moderate water movement and lighting and is usually non-aggressive so it can be located close to other flower animals. Photo by Dr. Elizabeth M. Wood.

ROOTED CORAL, *Turbinaria radicalis*, requires temperate water about 72°F. Moderate water movement, moderate lighting and growing space are its other requirements. This is a rare species with a very beautiful golden shade.

GOLDEN CUP CORAL,
***Turbinaria* species,**
requires slow water movement, moderate lighting and little growing space as it is not aggressive. Photo by Walt Deas.

SCROLL CORAL,
Turbinaria bifrons,
the Australian Cup coral, requires moderate water motion, moderate lighting and growing space.

CARIBBEAN ROSE *Manicina areolata,* as it is known in its rose-colored form. Photo by Dr. Patrick Colin.

PACIFIC ROSE CORAL, *Wellsophyllia radiata,* can only be positively identified by an examination of its unique skeleton. Otherwise it looks identical to *Manicina*. Requires moderate lighting, moderate water motion and is not territorial. Photo by Dr. Elizabeth M. Wood.

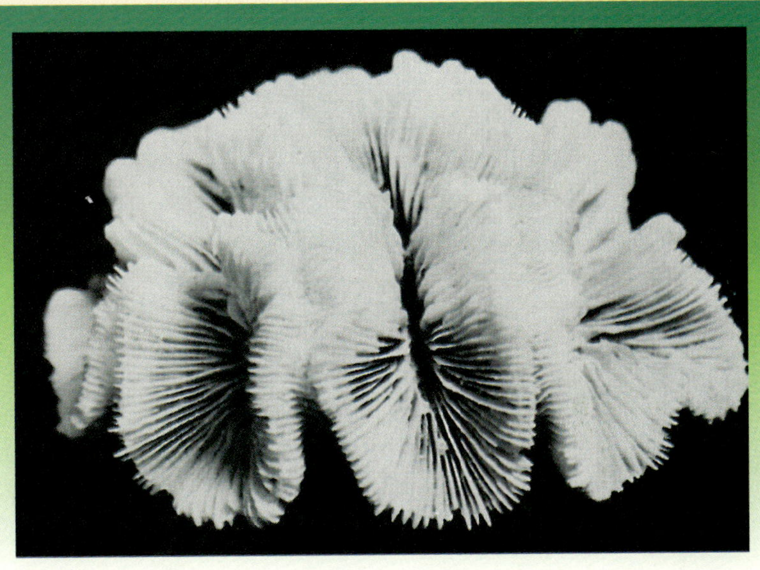

TONGUE CORAL, *Herpolitha limax,* requires moderate water movement, moderate lighting, some space around it so it can grow and an occasional feeding with crushed baby brine shrimp. The small round flower animal in the photo is a *Fungia*. Photo by Dr. Elizabeth M. Wood.

BROWN TONGUE CORAL, *Herpolitha weberi*, requires moderate water and light. It is fairly aggressive and should be fed once a month. There is a gall crab on this specimen. Photo by Dr. Leon P. Zann.

A close up of *Herpolitha limax*. Photo by Walt Deas.

SLIPPER CORAL, *Polyphyllia talpina*, requires moderate lighting, moderate water flow and a little room to grow. It can attack adjacent flower animals. Photo by Dr. Elizabeth M. Wood.

ATLANTIC SUN CORAL, ***Tubastrea coccinea,*** contains no zooxanthellae (algae) so it doesn't need much light. It does require a moderate water flow and is highly aggressive. Photo by Walt Deas.

ORANGE POLYP CORAL ***Tubastrea diaphana,*** has a very rare color. Low light, moderate water movement and lots of growing room are required. Photo by Walt Deas.

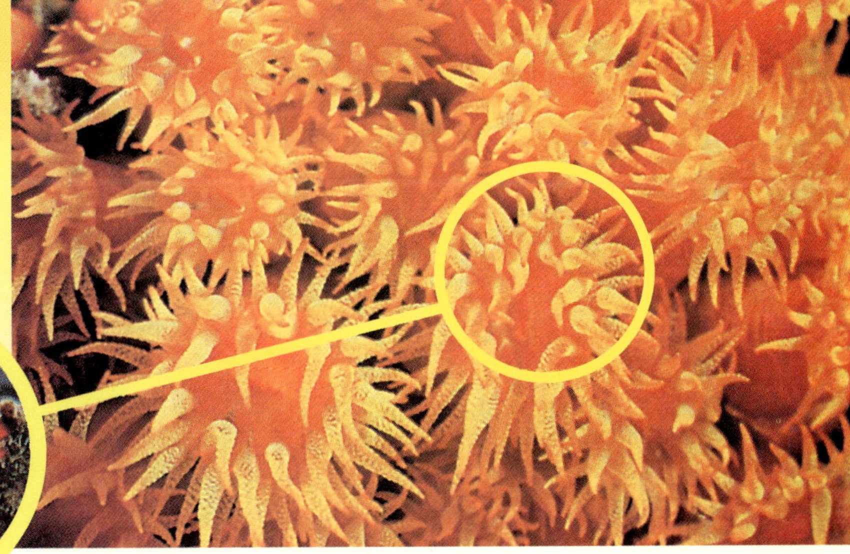

ORANGE SUN CORAL. ***Tubastrea aurea,*** This specimen was from Puerto Rico. The satellite photo shows the animal with its polyps retracted. Photos by Dr. Patrick Colin.

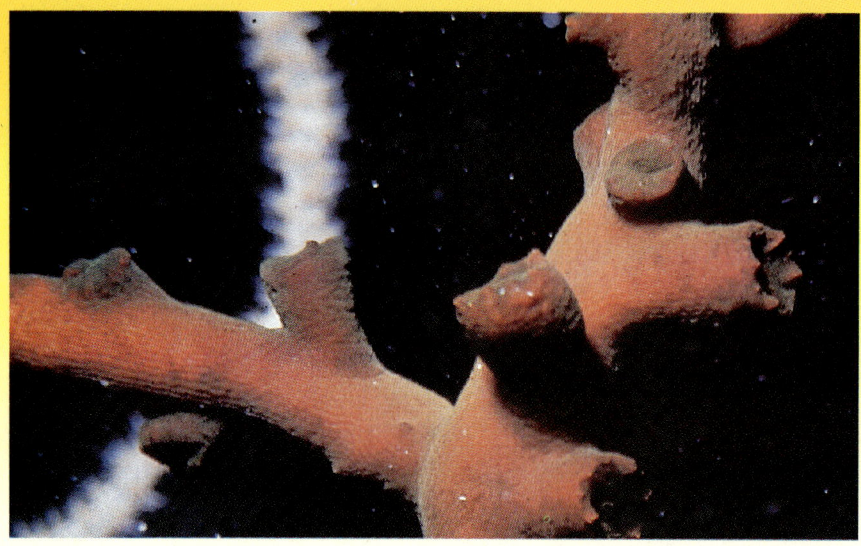

Black Sun Coral, *Tubastrea micrantha*, requires low light, moderate water movement and growing space. Photo by Walt Deas.

SUN CORAL *Tubastrea faulkneri*.

Two views of *Tubastrea faulkneri*. The Sun Coral doesn't need much light, but does need moderate water motion and growing space. Photos by Walt Deas.

Expanded polyps of *Tubastrea faulkneri*.

PIPE BRUSH CORAL, *Acropora formosa*, requires heavy lighting, substantial water movement and occasional feedings of living brine shrimp nauplii. It is fairly aggressive and requires attentive care. Photo by Walt Deas.

FLORIDA STAGHORN, *Acropora florida*, requires heavy lighting, heavy water movement and occasional feeding. It needs room to grow. Photo by Walt Deas.

PLATE STAGHORN CORAL, *Acropora* species, requires typically heavy lighting and water movement. It occasionally wants to be fed and requires growing room. Photo by Walt Deas.

ARMORED STAGHORN, *Acropora millepora*, requires heavy lighting and water movement. It needs room for growth. Photo by Walt Deas.

PINK STAGHORN, *Acropora humilis*, requires substantial lighting (10 hours a day), heavy water motion and growing space. Photo by Walt Deas.

STAGHORN,
Acropora,
It requires heavy lighting, very turbulent water and growing space. It is not recommended for the typical mini-reefer. Photo by Walt Deas.

AUSTRALIAN GREY,
Acropora
species,
the deep floor variety reproduces well from small pieces. It requires moderately heavy lighting, heavy water movements and adequate growing room.

CHINESE STAGHORN,
Acropora formosa,
retains its polyps during the daytime. It is an ideal hiding place for fishes and lobsters to say nothing of many invertebrates. It does well in the mini-reef for an experienced aquarist who can meet the demands of lots of light, massive movements of water and growing room.

GREEN STAGHORN *Acropora cervicornis,* from the Bahamas, is a great refuge for fishes. It requires heavy lighting and water motion, and can be fed every week or so. It is aggressive and requires space. Photo by Dr. Patrick Colin.

CAT'S PAW CORAL *Acropora prolifera,* This specimen is from the Bahamas. It requires 12 hours of strong, direct light, heavy water movement and growing space. Photo by Dr. Patrick Colin.

This is the way a Staghorn coral grows on a protected reef slope. It takes over everything. Photo by Dr. Patrick Colin.

The polyps of Staghorn corals are very small. This is a night picture when the polyps are emerged. Photo by Walt Deas.

THE REDBERRY STAGHORN,
Acropora valida,
is the most desirable of all Staghorns. It requires constant warm temperatures of at least 80 ° F, constantly moving water and the equivalent of 8 hours of sunlight per day. Photo by Walt Deas.

PINK STAGHORN
Acropora nobilis,
Requires heavy lighting and water movements. They need room to grow.

Acropora hyacinthus, the Hyacinth Coral (above), and *Acropora loripes*, the Bluetip Coral (below), have the same requirements of 8 hours of sunlight or the equivalent, constant rapid water movement and growing space. Photos by Walt Deas.

Seriatopora hystrix with crab galls. The crab forces the coral to form a cage around the female crab who spends the rest of her life as a prisoner of the coral. The males are much smaller than the female and they can enter or leave the gall without difficulty. Photo by Walt Deas.

BRUSH CORAL, ***Seriatopora caliendrum,*** requires heavy lighting, heavy water movement and minimal separation from other flower animals. If you can supply the physical needs, the animal will prosper; if you can't, the animal will probably perish. Photo by Walt Deas.

BIRD'S NEST CORAL, ***Seriatopora hystrix,*** grows close to the surface in nature so it needs 8 hours of sunlight per day, plus turbulent water and lots of room to grow. It is extremely difficult to keep alive if these conditions are not supplied. If, however, you can supply the necessary conditions, it will thrive. Photos of *Seriatopora hystrix* by Dr. Elizabeth M. Wood.

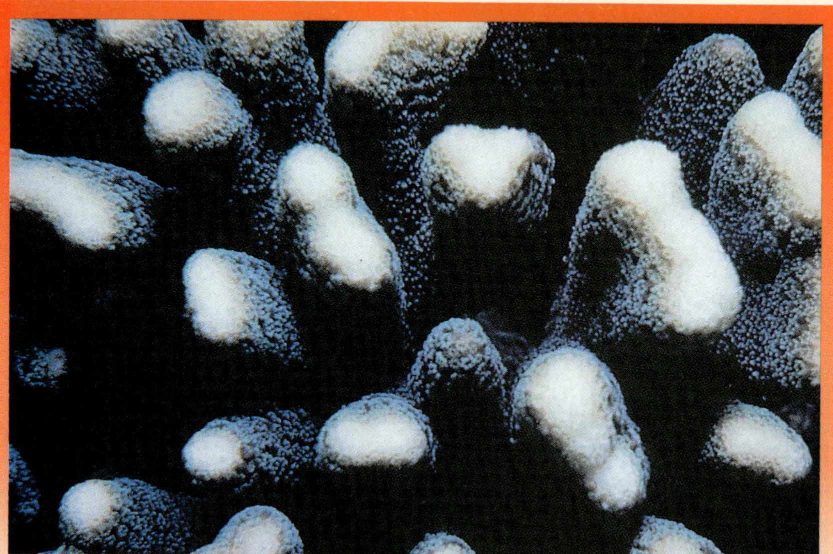

CLUBFOOT CORAL OR THE GYPSY CORAL, ***Stylophora pistillata,*** is very difficult to care for and only very experienced mini-reefers should attempt to keep them alive. They require 12 hours of sunlight, heavy water movements and a little growing room. Photo by Walt Deas.

Stylophora pistillata. Photo by Walt Deas.

LETTUCE CLUMP CORAL, ***Pavona venosa,*** requires heavy lighting, heavy water motion and lots of growing space. Photo by Walt Deas.

CACTUS CORAL, *Pavona decussata*,

requires 10 hours of sunlight or its equivalent, heavy water movement and some growing room.

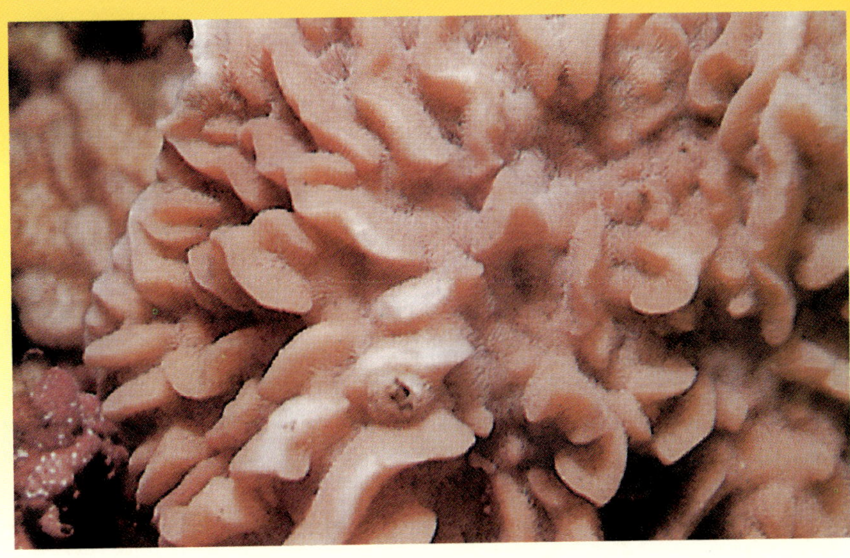

Pavona decussata.
Photo by Walt Deas.

CACTUS COLUMN CORAL, *Pavona clavus*,

This specimen is from Sabah, Malaysia. It requires 8 hours of sunlight or its equivalent (if there is such a thing!), heavy water movement and some growing room.

Pavona decussata. Photo by Dr. Elizabeth M Wood.

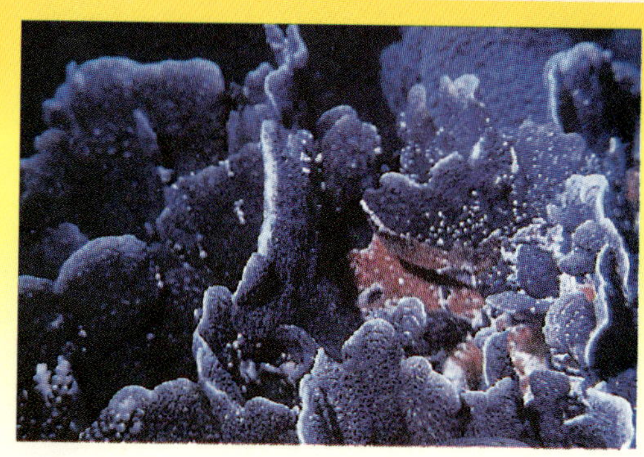

Pavona decussata.

Walt Deas with *Pavona minuta*. This species has not been kept in a mini-reef aquarium but does well in very large tanks under the same parameters as other *Pavona* species. Photo by Jean Deas.

FRILLY CACTUS, ***Pavona cactus,*** requires 8 hours of sunlight (or its equivalent), heavy water motion, and just a bit of room for expansion as it is not aggressive. It grows in heavy patches when you are successful. Photo by Walt Deas.

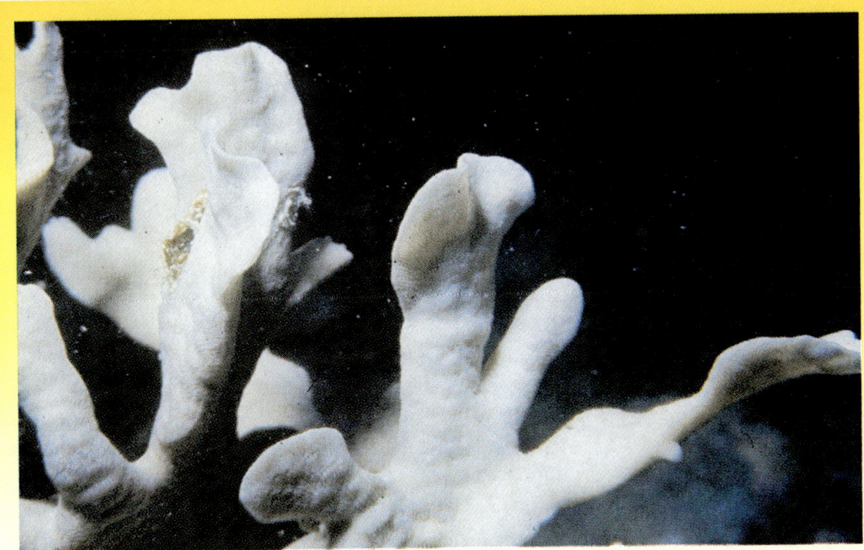

BRAIN CACTUS CORAL, ***Pavona varians,*** demands 10 hours sunlight (or equivalent) and very active water motions to survive. It is a test coral for beginners who think they have the know-how to advance with a more difficult species. Photo by Walt Deas.

DRIED POTATO CACTUS, ***Pavona* species,** with the same requirements as *Pavona varians.* Photos by Walt Deas.

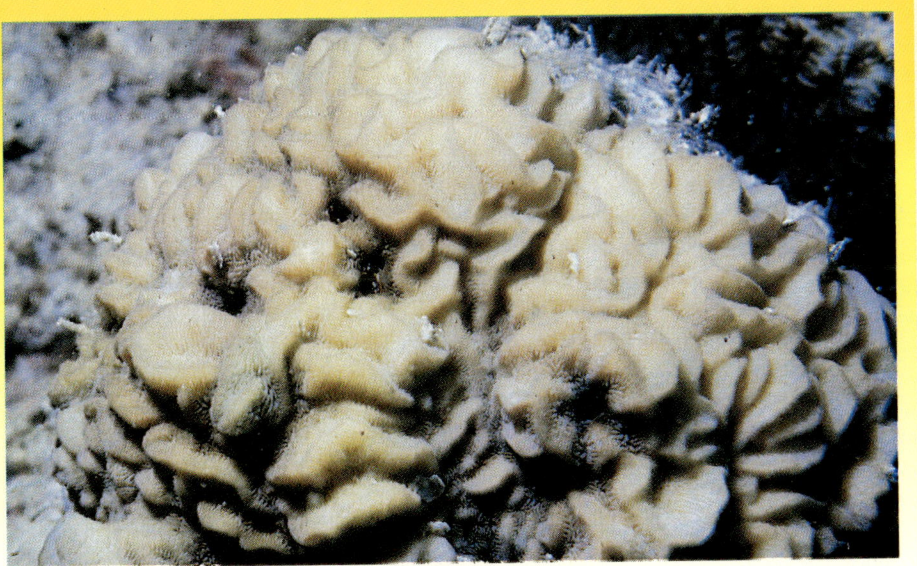

HORN CORALS
Hydnophora rigida.

Even more difficult to maintain successfully is the most popular *species Hydnophora rigida*, the Horn Coral, which looks like a tangled mass similar to the *Acropora*. They require 8 hours of very bright lighting, heavy water agitation and they are terribly aggressive. They usually destroy any flower animal with which they make contact. Photo by Dr. Elizabeth M. Wood.

KNOB HORN CORAL,
Hydnophora pilosa,

is only for advanced mini-reefers. It requires heavy lighting and water movement. It cannot be close to other corals as it kills them. Photos by Dr. Elizabeth M. Wood.

HORNY BRANCH CORAL,
Hydnophora exesa,

requires 10 hours of sunlight or its equivalent, rapid water movement and isolation for growth. Photo by Walt Deas.

YELLOW HORN CORAL,
Hydnophora microconus,
is the most compatible species in the genus for the mini-reefer. It needs lots of intense light and water movement, but it thrives if these physical requirements are supplied. You still have to have a lot of experience with corals to succeed with any of the horn corals. Photos by Dr. Elizabeth M. Wood and Walt Deas

JEWEL CORALS,
***Porites* species,**
are very difficult to maintain and are not recommended for the beginner. When beginners are ready to try their skills on more difficult flower animals, this is the genus to tackle. They need 10-12 hours of bright light every day with very heavy water movement. They can stand crowding and are not a danger to their coral neighbors. They have been called *jewel* corals because their corallites look like jewels to some people (not to me!). Photo by Walt Deas.

BLUE JEWEL CORAL,

***Porites* species,**
does not require as much light as the other *Porites*, but it does need 6-8 hours of bright light per day with lots of water movement. Photo by MP&C Piednoir Aqua Press.

GOLDEN JEWEL CORAL, *Porites* species, is found in very shallow water in a protected reef area. This species needs lots of light (10 hours of sunlight per day), but not too much water agitation. Photo by Walt Deas.

FINGER JEWEL CORAL, *Porites cylindrica*, with diver Jean Deas to show the massiveness of this coral head. It requires lots of light and water movement as do most of the members of this genus. Photo by Walt Deas.

HAND JEWEL CORAL, *Porites annae*, does fairly well with some experts and poorly with others. Some beginners even have success...*beginner's luck*, they say. In any case they don't do well without 8-10 hours of direct sunlight (or its equivalent), massive movements of water and the company of small fishes. Photo by Walt Deas.

Porites lutea with Christmas Tree Worms, *Spirobranchus giganteus,* has earned this *Porites* the name Christmas Tree Worm Rock. Unfortunately there are many such corals in the genus as these worms select any *Porites* available. As the *Porites* is so difficult to maintain, so are the worms which infect them. When the coral dies so do the worms! These worms are also referred to as Feather Duster Worms; they are very sensitive and irregular water movements, strong light or sounds makes them withdraw. Photo by Cathy Church.

JEWELED TOE CORAL, ***Porites antennuata,*** has the same harsh requirements as most *Porites*. Heavy water movements, 10-12 hours of sunlight or its equivalent in artificial lighting, and no demands on living space are requirements to maintain this flower animal. Photo by Walt Deas.

Porites **and** ***Millepora*** can thrive together. Photo by Walt Deas.

FINGER JEWEL CORAL. ***Porites cylindrica,*** Photo by Walt Deas.

TURTLE JEWEL CORAL, *Porites lobata*, is extremely difficult to maintain in the mini-reef aquarium. It requires 12 hours of sunlight or its artificial equivalent and heavy water motion. It is not aggressive but I have only seen it successfully cultivated in large public aquariums which have running sea water. Photo by Walt Deas.

CHRISTMAS TREE WORM ROCK, *Porites lutea*, is the preferred *Porites* for the Christmas Tree Worm, *Spirobranchus giganteus*. Photo by Walt Deas.

CAULIFLOWER, WART CORAL
Pocillopora damicornis

An amazing photo, it shows a gall crab *Hapalocarcinus marsupialis* entrapped for its lifetime in the tip of the branch of *Pocillopora damicornis* coral. The male gall crabs are small enough to crawl in and out of the slit in the coral tip to mate with the female. Photo by Dr. Elizabeth M. Wood.

CAULIFLOWER CORAL
Pocillopora damicornis,

It requires 8 hours of bright light and very heavy water movement. It should not be adjacent to any other flower animals. Photo by Dr. Gerald R. Allen and Roger Steene.

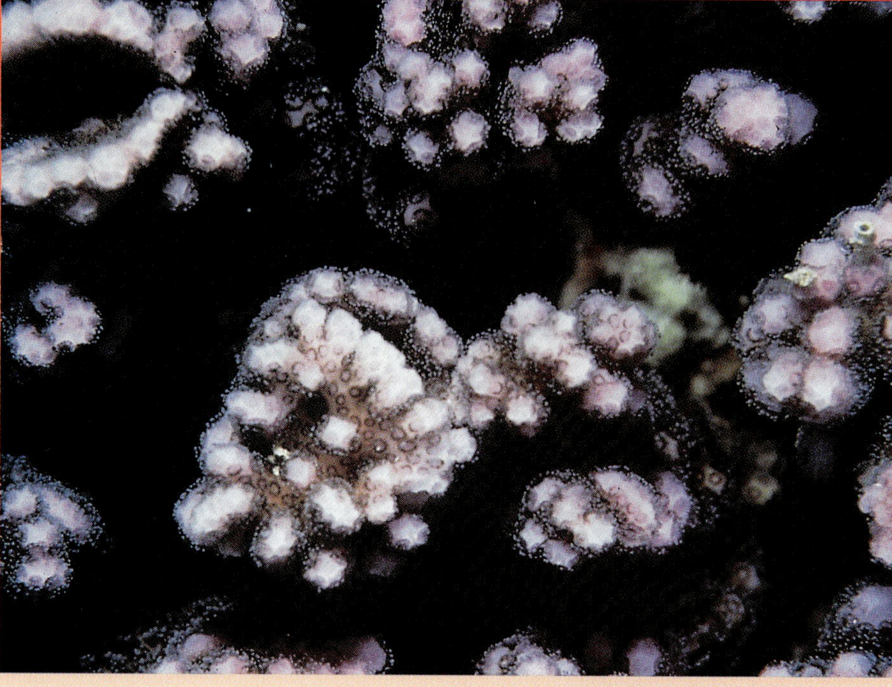

CAULIFLOWER CORAL
Pocillopora damicornis,

with two crab galls. Photo by Walt Deas.

BLUSHING CAULIFLOWER CORAL, ***Pocillopora* species,** is very difficult to maintain in captivity...but so were all corals in 1980! This one requires lots of light, up to 12 hours a day, and heavy water movement. It should not be adjacent to other flower animals. Photo by Walt Deas.

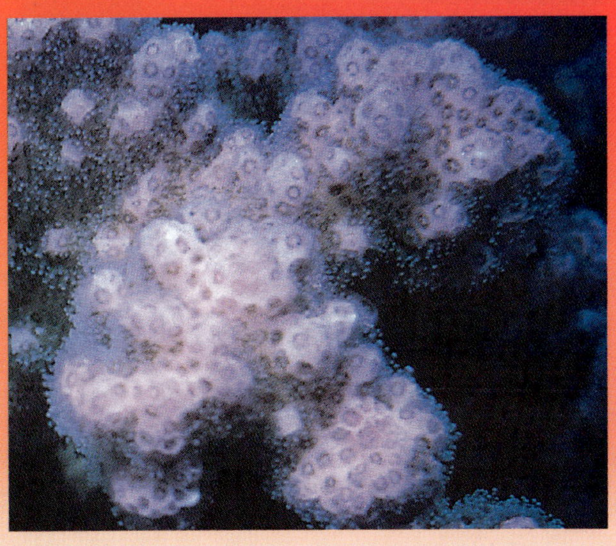

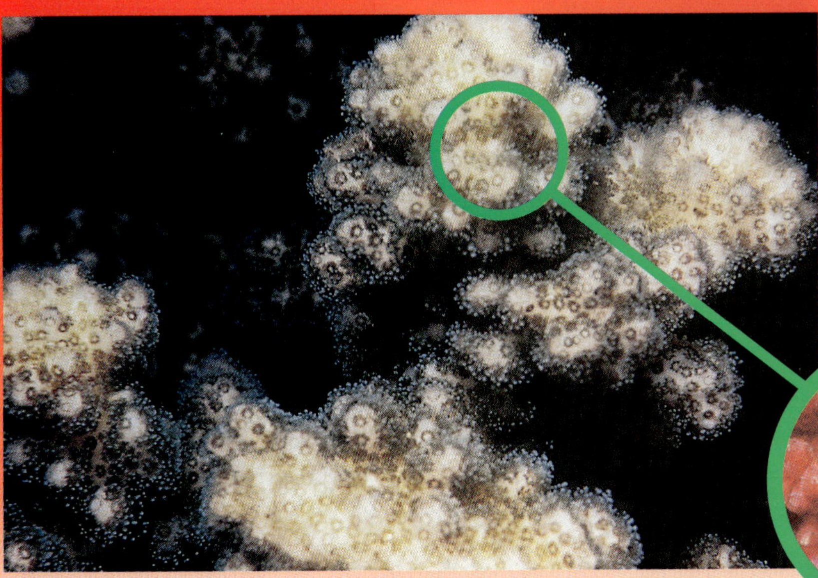

PINK CAULIFLOWER, ***Pocillopora verrucosa,*** requires 10 hours of intense light and heavy water movement. It should not be adjacent to other flower animals. Photo by Walt Deas.

PINK CAULIFLOWER, ***Pocillopora verrucosa,*** *is not always pink!* Photo by Dr. Elizabeth M. Wood.

PINK WART CAULIFLOWER CORAL *Pocillopora* species, requires 10 hours of intense light and heavy water movements. It is very difficult to maintain for long periods of time probably because of its need for certain trace elements, but this is just speculation on my part.

GOLD CARNATION CORAL, *Pectinia* species, needs 8 hours of intense light and fairly heavy water movements, but it is still the most difficult of corals to maintain in the mini-reef aquarium. Photo by Dr. Elizabeth M. Wood.

ANTLER LETTUCE, *Pectinia alcicornis*, requires 10 hours of intense light per day and heavy water movement. Like all *Pectinia*, this is a difficult flower animal to maintain. Photo by Dr. Elizabeth M. Wood.

WITHERED LETTUCE, *Pectinia* species from Sabah, Malaysia, requires the same care as *Pectinia alcicornis*. Photo by Dr. Elizabeth M. Wood.

HIBISCUS LETTUCE CORAL, *Pectinia paeonia*, is very difficult to maintain as are all *Pectinia*. Heavy water movement and 10 hours of intense lighting are minimal requirements, but they are not an aggressive species. Photo by Dr. Elizabeth M. Wood.

FRILLY LETTUCE OR CARNATION CORAL, *Pectinia lactuca*, is difficult to maintain. It must have 10 hours of intense light per day and heavy water movement constantly. Photo by MP&C Piednoir Aqua Press.

FRILLY LETTUCE CORAL, The skeleton of *Pectinia lactuca*, is just as beautiful as the living animal. Skeletons are necessary to verify identifications. Photo by Dr. Herbert R. Axelrod.

SALAD BOWL CORAL, ***Montipora capricornis,*** occurs in very deep waters as well as in depths of 15-20 feet. But their mini-reef aquarium needs are the same: 8-10 hours of intense light daily. Photo by Walt Deas.

SALAD BOWL CORAL, ***Montipora capricornis,*** in its foliaceous form. This coral appears in other forms as well but they all require 8-10 hours of intense light per day, moderate water movement and can safely be adjacent to other flower animals. Photo by Dr. Elizabeth M. Wood.

SALAD BOWL CORAL ***Montipora capricornis,*** Photo by Walt Deas.

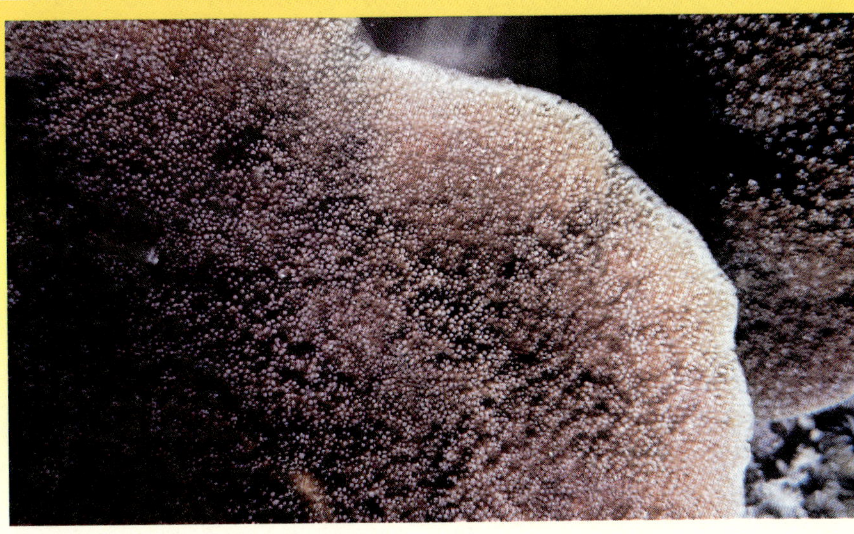

Montipora stellata. Photo by Walt Deas.

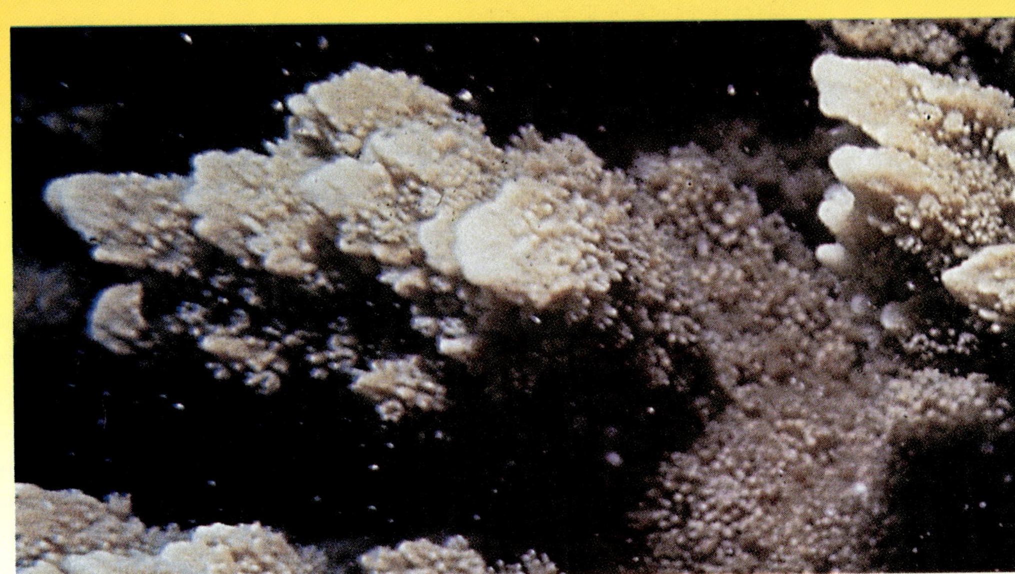

Montipora stellata. Photo by Walt Deas.

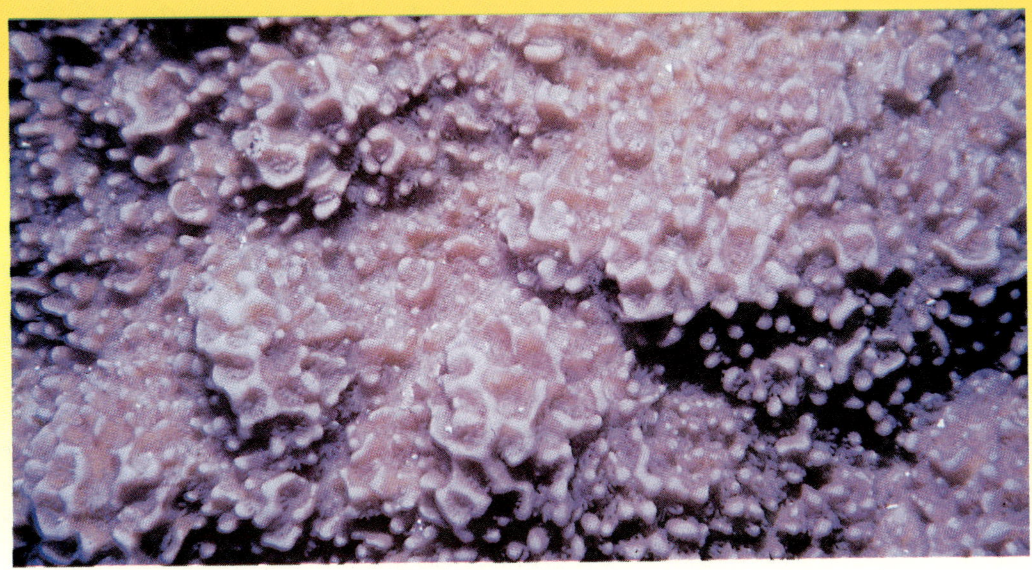

Montipora verrucosa. Photo by Walt Deas.

VELVET FINGER CORAL, *Montipora digitata,*

is a delicate coral and the fingers break easily making it difficult to transport. It requires 7 hours of strong light per day with substantial water movement.

These leafy and plate-like corals found in 20 feet of water in Sabah, Malaysia are called *Montipora spongodes*, the Velvet Stone Coral or Velvet Lump Coral. They require 9 hours of strong light per day, moderate water movement and can tolerate neighboring flower animals. Photos by Dr. Elizabeth M. Wood and Walt Deas.

VELVET FINGER CORAL, *Montipora digitata,*

with its polyps extended.

VELVET CORAL, *Montipora verrucosa,* requires 9 hours of strong light with moderate water motion. It is not aggressive. Photo by Walt Deas.

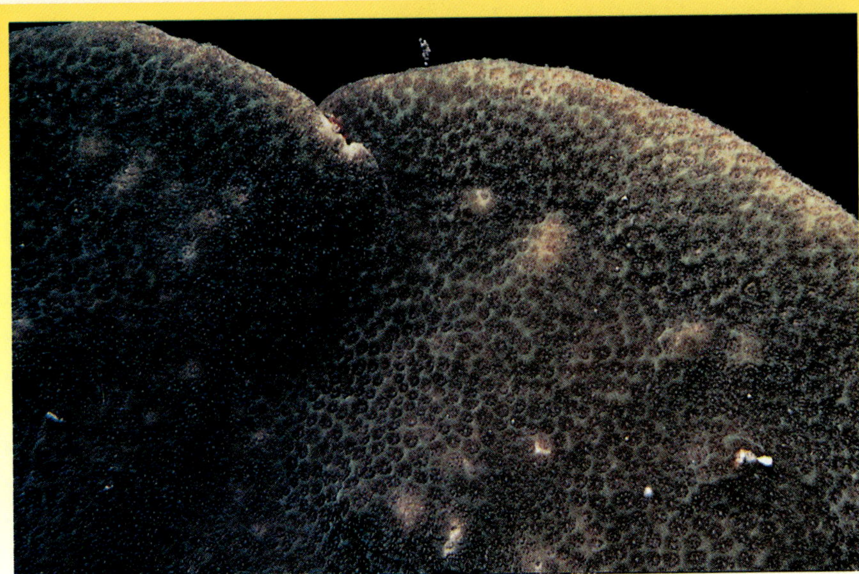

VELVET STONE CORAL, *Montipora spongodes,* requires 9 hours of light and moderate water movement. While it is a difficult flower animal to maintain in an aquarium, it flourishes for some mini-reefers who can't explain the reason for their success. Photo by Walt Deas.

PURPLE VELVET CORAL, *Montipora grisea,* requires standard care for the velvets with 8-10 hours of strong light and moderate water motion. Photo by Walt Deas.

RUFFLED CORAL, ***Merulina ampliata,*** requires turbid water and 8 hours of direct sunlight. Photos by Dr. Elizabeth M. Wood.

TAN RUFFLED CORAL, ***Merulina scabricula,*** is extremely difficult to maintain unless you give it 10 hours of sunlight (or its artificial equivalent) and moderately heavy water movement. It doesn't bother other flower animals. Photo by Walt Deas.

***Merulina* species,** simply called Merulina in the trade, requires the same care as *scabricula*.

STARLET CORAL, *Solenastrea bournoni*, is the mini-reefer's dream. It is beautiful, hardy, not fussy about lighting which can be as low as two hours daily (though 8 hours is better), very moderate water movement and only moderately aggressive. It is very suitable for beginners. Photo by Dr. Elizabeth M. Wood.

Montastrea annularis is usually mistaken for *Solenastrea bournoni* in the trade, but it doesn't matter since both are beautiful and both are easily cared for. Light water motion and 4-8 hours of strong light. Photo by Dr. Elizabeth M. Wood.

Jean Deas on the Great Barrier Reef helping to identify the photos in this book!

PIPE ORGAN CORAL SKELETON, *Tubipora musica*,

This non-scleractinian coral does build reef. . . A rare trait. Photo by Dr. Herbert R. Axelrod.

Unexpanded polyps of *Tubipora musica*. Photo by Walt deas.

NON-SCLERACTINIAN CORALS

These are the soft corals which usually do not build reefs through the utilization of their hard skeletons. They are very popular in mini-reef aquariums and their skeletons are also very interesting. Some of their skeletons are even colored!

Many of these non-scleractinian corals are cave corals which are hidden from the rays of the sun, thus they do not contain the symbiotic algae we call *zooxanthellae*. Thus these corals must be fed with freshly hatched brine shrimp, unless there are enough fishes in the mini-reef tank to generate fish waste upon which these corals can subsist.

The feared fire corals with their dangerous stinging tentacles, belonging to the genus *Millepora*, belong to this group. Obviously they should be handled with care. All corals should be handled with gloved hands, even if you think they do not sting.

1.

2.

3.

1. *Tubipora musica,* The Pipe Organ Coral
2. *Millepora alcicornis,* The Fire Coral
3. *Stylaster species*

PIPE ORGAN CORAL, ***Tipora musica,*** is a delight in the aquarium. It is easy to care for if you give it lots of light, plenty of water movement and an occasional feeding of newly hatched brine shrimp.

PIPE ORGAN CORAL ***Tubipora musica,*** requires heavy lighting, heavy aeration and moderate space.

FIRE CORAL, ***Millepora alcicornis,*** has stinging tentacles and stinging cells in its polyps. It requires an experienced aquarist to keep it alive and healthy. It needs heavy lighting, moderate turbulence and complete isolation from other corals. DON'T TOUCH THIS CORAL WITH YOUR BARE HANDS! Photo by Walt Deas.

FIRE CORAL, *Millepora tenella*, is neither easy nor safe in the mini-reef aquarium, but challenges are what makes the hobby so interesting. Heavy lighting, moderate water movement and isolation because it kills its neighboring flower animals. Photo by Walt Deas.

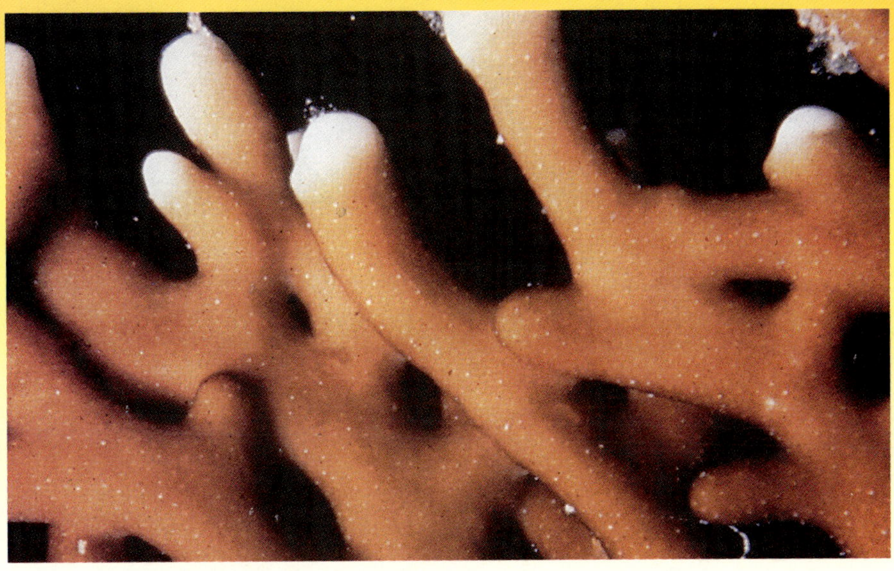

Millepora tenella.

PLATE FIRE CORAL, *Millepora platyphyllia*, is a nasty animal that truly stings. In the mini-reef aquarium it requires separation from other corals, moderate aeration and lots of light. Photo by Walt Deas.

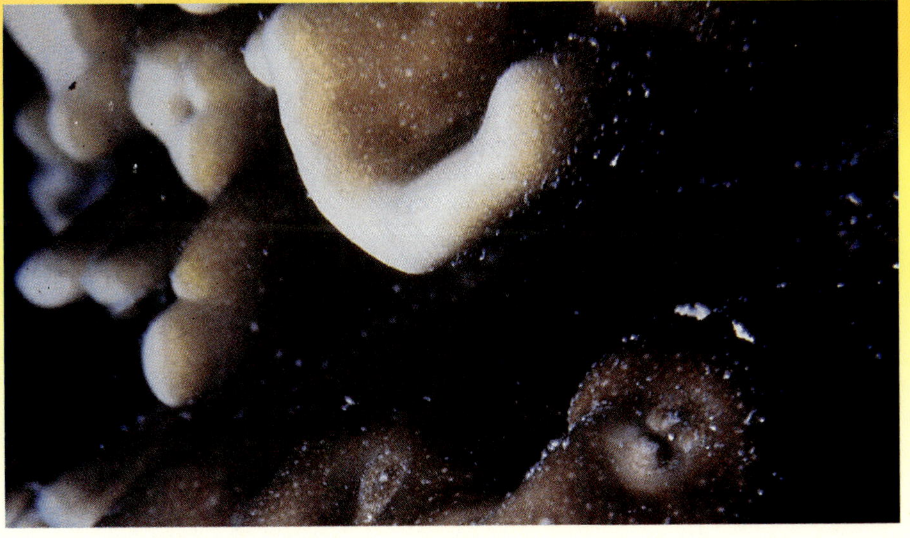

***Stylaster* species** requires normal light, slow water movements and is highly territorial so keep it isolated. It does not thrive under many mini-reef situations but it is worth a try. Photo by Walt Deas.

***Stylaster* species** which needs normal lighting, slow water movements and isolation. Photo by Walt Deas.

GLOWING EMBER CORAL *Distichopora violacea* from Eniwetok. Photo by Scott Johnson.

LEATHER & SOFT CORALS

Leather corals are extremely popular with minireefers because of the ease with which they acclimate to life in the mini-reef tank. Because of their symbiotic relationship with algae which live in the cells of their polyps, food is not required, though occasional feedings of newly hatched brine shrimp can't hurt if the tank has fishes to gobble up the uneaten shrimps.

While very hardy, they do shed their outer skins or slime coatings. These sloughed off coatings can smother other corals so be observant.

The natural habitat of these corals is that part of the reef which doesn't get pounded with water. This means they live in lagoons and this shallow habitat is also safe from larger, reef-chewing fishes.

They do require salt water of high quality with the complete range of trace elements. The elements iodine and strontium are especially necessary to the corals in this group.

1. *Alcyonium*
2. *Cladiella*
3. *Sarcophyton acutangulum*

ENCRUSTING SOFT CORAL, *Alcyonium* species, is easily maintained with 6 hours of light and moderate water movement. This species may be *fulvum*. Photo by Dr. Gerald R. Allen & Roger Steene.

RED CHILI CORAL, *Alcyonium* species, requires moderate lighting, moderate water movement and space to grow. It is a good species for beginners who have the ability to supply the physical needs of this species. Photo by Rodney Jonklaas of a Sri Lankan variety.

LEATHER CORAL, *Sarcophyton trocheliphorum*, is an easy coral for the beginner. It requires only 4 hours of intense light per day and light water movements. It is very aggressive and should not be placed near other flower animals. Photo by MP&C Piednoir Aqua Press.

LEATHER CORAL, *Sarcophyton trocheliphorum*, is an easy coral for the beginner. It requires only 4 hours of intense light per day and light water movements. It is very aggressive and should not be placed near other flower animals. Photo by MP&C Piednoir Aqua Press.

A fully grown *Sarcophyton trocheliphorum*. Photo by Walt Deas.

SOFT CORAL, MUSHROOM LEATHER CORAL, *Sarcophyton acutangulum*, is easily maintained with slowly moving water and 4 hours of intense light daily. Photo by Dr. Gerald R. Allen and Roger Steene.

MUSHROOM CORAL, *Sarcophyton lobulatum*, is easily maintained with moderate water movement and 4-5 hours daily intense lighting. Photo by Walt Deas.

Sarcophyton molle is easily maintained with moderate water flow and 4 hours of direct intense light. Photo by Walt Deas.

GOLDEN CROWN TOADSTOOL CORAL, *Sarcophyton glaucum*, is easy to maintain with moderate lighting and moderate water flow. Photo by Walt Deas.

EHRENBERG'S MUSHROOM CORAL, *Sarcophyton ehrenbergi*, is simple to maintain with moderate light and water flow. Photo by Dr. Elizabeth M. Wood.

CABBAGE CORAL, *Lobophyton pauciflorum*, is for beginners with a minimum of 3 hours intense lighting per day and slow to moderate water flows. Photo by Walt Deas.

FLOWER LEATHER CORAL, *Lobophyton crassum*, has minimum needs of 3 hours of intense, direct light and slow-moving waters bathing it. Photo by Walt Deas.

MEDUSA TREE CORAL,
Sphaerella krempfi,
needs a few hours of intense lighting and moderate water currents. It is not aggressive. Photo by Dr. Herbert R. Axelrod.

CARROT-LEATHER CORAL
Carotalcyon sagamianum,
requires moderate water flows and

MEDUSA TREE CORAL,
Sphaerella krempfi,
is gorgeous but needs a few hours of direct strong lighting and moderate water movement. Photo by U. Erich Friese.

***Sinularia* species** are difficult to identify. *Sinularia* are simple to care for in the mini-reef aquarium. They need 4-6 hours of light and strong water movement. Photos by U.Erich Friese

***Sinularia* species**

GOLD FINGER CORAL, *Sinularia macropodia*, requires little care other than 4-6 hours of intense lighting and moderate water movement. Photo by Walt Deas.

WHITE FINGER CORAL, *Sinularia asterolobata*, is also called the Snow Coral. It is simple to care for with 4 hours direct light and moderate water movement. Photo by Walt Deas.

TREE CORAL, *Nephthea* species, requires light because it contains zooxanthellae, 6 hours a day with moderate water movement. It should also be fed once a week with newly hatched brine shrimp. Photo by MP&C Piednoir Aqua Press.

COLT CORAL *Cladiella* species are excellent for starting mini-reefers. They may well be one of the most accommodating of the corals but they are very difficult to identify. It doesn't matter, they are all the same as far as care is concerned. Lighting is not important, They are also not fussy about water movement and they can tolerate little or a lot of water motion. This is a colt coral thriving in a home aquarium. Photo by Glen S. Axelrod.

GOLD CARNATION, *Dendronephthya aurea*, is not for beginners. They require little light and not much of a water flow but they rarely live for a year in the average well-managed mini-reef aquarium.

WHITE CARNATION CORAL, *Dendronephthya mirabelis*, requires room light because they do not contain zooxanthellae (symbiotic algae), a moderate water movement and can be positioned close to other flower animals. Photo by Walt Deas.

SPIKE CARNATION *Dendronephthya* species, require little light, moderate water movement and weekly feedings of mashed brine shrimp. Photos by Walt Deas.

SPIKE CARNATION *Dendronephthya* species, require little light, moderate water movement and weekly feedings of mashed brine shrimp. Photos by Walt Deas.

VIOLACEOUS CARNATION, *Dendronephthya* species, does not require special lighting as it does not contain symbiotic algae (zooxanthellae). Light water movement and weekly feedings are required, but it is still hard to maintain successfully. Photo by Walt Deas.

PINK CARNATION *Dendronephthya* species, also called the Pink Carnation as some three other species are, has little light requirements as it does not contain symbiotic algae. Moderate water movement is appreciated. Photo by Walt Deas.

Two *Dendronephthya* species. The photo above shows the Golden Carnation while the lower photo shows the Blood Red Carnation. Both are difficult to maintain. But they thrive in low lighting situations with moderate water movement. Photos by Walt Deas.

Paralemnalia species shown above is called the Brown Carnation and *Scleronephthya* species shown below is known as the Orange Carnation. Both do not contain algae so they have no real need for bright lighting. They are fond of moderately moving water but still are not for beginning mini-reefers. Photos by Walt Deas.

WARTY SOFT CORAL,
***Scleronephthya* species,**
contains no symbiotic algae therefore does not require bright lighting. It thrives under moderate water movement and weekly feedings of newly hatched brine shrimp. Photo by Walt Deas.

A magnificent underwater scene showing *Xenia* pulsing corals in the Philippine Islands. These require substantial water movement, 8 hours or so of intense lighting and they can be located close to other flower animals. Photo by MP&C Piednoir Aqua Press.

OCTOPUS CORAL, *Cespitularia* species have eight tentacles and sometimes they pulse. They are not difficult to maintain if the specimen has not be damaged in transit. They require 8 hours of intense light per day, high water movement and some space to grow. Photo by Dr. L.P.Zann.

TABBY PULSING CORAL, *Xenia* species, requires heavy water movement and substantial lighting at least 8 hours per day. Photo by Walt Deas.

UMBRELLA XENIA, ***Xenia umbellata,*** is the prettiest of the Xenia. It needs heavy water movement and intense lighting for 9 hours per day. Photo by Walt Deas.

Closely related to the familiar *Xenia* is the *Heteroxenia* species called the False Xenia Coral, they are easier to maintain than *Xenia*. They need 8 hours intense lighting, heavy water movements and can be crowded. Photo by Walt Deas.

Minabae aldersladei, sometimes referred to as the Pom-pon Xenia, has the same requirements as *Heteroxenia*. The scientific name of this species has not been confirmed but was supplied by the photographer. In any case, it is closely related to *Xenia*.

WEDDING VEIL XENIA, ***Xenia puertogalerae,*** requires 8 hours of direct lighting and heavy water movement to thrive. Photo by Walt Deas.

Xenia elongata. Photo by Keith Gillette.

GIANT ANTHELIA, ***Anthelia glauca,*** requires 9 hours of intense lighting and heavy water movement. Photo by Dr. Leon P. Zann.

WAVING HAND CORAL, *Anthelia* species, requires 8 hours of intense lighting per day with actively moving water. Photo by Dr. Leon P. Zann.

GOLDEN BUTTON CORAL, *Zoanthus* species, are highly recommended for beginners. They have minimal lighting needs and 3 hours of intense lighting per day is sufficient. Moderate water movement and little growing space rounds out their needs.

GREEN MOON POLYP CORAL, *Palythoa* species, is easy to care for with 5 hours intense lighting, moderate water motion and some room to grow. Photo by U. Erich Friese.

OLIVE ENCRUSTING CORAL, ***Zoanthus*** **species,** needs little light (2 hours per day of intense lighting) and moderate water motion. Photo by U. Erich Friese.

GREEN SEA MAT CORAL, ***Palythoa,*** requires 4 hours of direct intense light, moderate water motion and little room for growth. Photo by U. Erich Friese.

GOLDEN SEA MAT CORAL, ***Zoanthus*** **species,** is easily cared for in the mini-reef aquarium. It requires 3 hours of intense light and a moderate flow of water around it. Photo by U. erich Friese.

GREEN BUTTON SEA MAT,
Zoanthus pulchellus,
is ideal for the beginner. Only 2 hours of intense lighting, moderate water movement and not too much space are the requirements. I've never seen this species fail in the mini-reef tank if these physical conditions are supplied. This species has also been placed in the genus *Palythoa.* Photo by U. Erich Friese.

LONG-HAIRED SEA MAT,
***Zoanthus* species,**
is easy to care for. Just 2 hours of intense lighting per day and moderate water movement are required. Photo by MP&C Piednoir Aqua Press.

BALLET DANCER CORAL,
Parazoanthus gracilis,
is not difficult to care for. It requires 3-4 hours of direct, intense lighting per day plus moderate water motion through its tentacles. Photo by U. Erich Friese.

OCTOCORAL, *Telesto* species, requires 3 hours of intense lighting and room to grow as it is a fast grower under ideal conditions.

GREEN STAR POLYPS CORAL, *Clavularia viridis*, is simple to care for with 5 hours of intense lighting and a moderate flow of water over the entire flower animal. Photo by MP&C Piednoir Aqua Press.

CHRISTMAS TREE POLYP CORAL, *Carijoa* species, a member of the family Clavulariidae, requires 8 hours of intense light per day and moderate water movement. Photo by Walt Deas.

ORANGE SEA FAN *Melithaea* species,

from the Red Sea, Requires back lighting and top lighting, feeding, modest water movement and expertise in mini-reef management. They do best in a tank by themselves. Photo by MP&C Piednoir.

GOLDEN SEA FAN *Melithaea Acabaria*,

from Australia, requires the same care as all *Melithaea* with top and back lighting. They do best in a tank by themselves. Photo by Walt Deas.

FRILLED SEA FAN, *Melithaea ochracea*,

requires back and top lighting and technical support including special filtration. Certainly not recommended for the beginner. Photo by Walt Deas.

***Melithaea* species** from the Red Sea are easily removed and shipped but they do not thrive under ordinary mini-reef conditions. Photo by MP&C Piednoir Aqua Press.

***Acanthogorgia* species** are magnificent and entice mini-reefers to maintain them in their homes, but they have special requirements which are best served in their own, separate aquarium. Photo by Walt Deas.

***Melithaea* species** magnificent and greatly entice mini-reefers to maintain them in their homes, but they have special requirements which are best served in their own, separate aquarium. Photo by Walt Deas.

FEATHER STAR ON AN ORANGE SEA FAN

Photo by Walt Deas.

GOLDEN GORGONIA, *Subergorgia mollis*,

can be successfully maintained using the drip method of constantly adding new water with replenished trace elements. But they require back lighting as well as top lighting and, essentially, do best in their own mini-reef tank. Photo by Walt Deas.

Melithaea species,

similar to *Acanthogorgia*, has been successfully maintained in the mini-reef tank following the instructions for sea fans. Photo by Walt Deas.

GOLDEN SEA FAN, ***Melithaea acabaria,*** in its not-so-golden phase. Photo by Walt Deas.

DEEP WATER SEA FAN, ***Melithaea* species.** A Brittle Star on a deep water (200 feet) *Melithaea* species. The deep water species seem to do better in the mini-reef tank because they require very little light. Photo by Walt Deas.

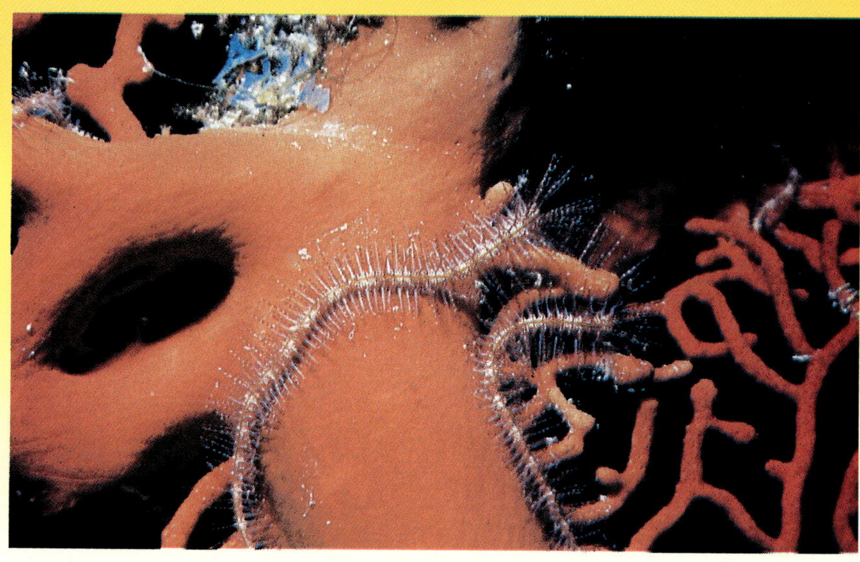

RED-VEINED SEA FAN, ***Melithaea* species,** also seems to do well in the mini-reef tank but requires expert care especially as far as lighting is concerned. Photo by Walt Deas.

CHRISTMAS SEA FAN, *Melithaea* species are difficult to care for and require back and top lighting as well as uniform water movement and are best maintained in their own mini-reef aquarium.

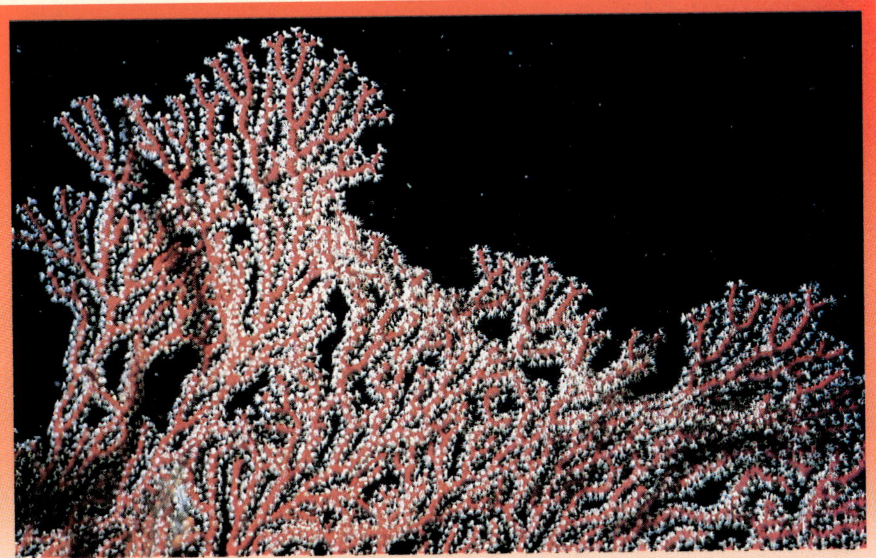

YELLOW-SPOTTED SEA FAN, *Acanthogorgia* species difficult to care for and require back and top lighting as well as uniform water movement and are best maintained in their own mini-reef aquarium. Photo by MP&C Piednoir.

GOLDEN GORGONIAN *Subergorgia* species Difficult to maintain but you have a chance if you carefully follow the instructions in the text. Photos by Walt Deas.

GOLDEN SEA FAN
Melithaea acabaria,
in its yellow phase. Difficult to maintain but you have a chance if you carefully follow the instructions in the text. Photos by Walt Deas.

The Gorgonian Crab, *Xenocarcinus depressus* scavenges the Blushing Sea Fan, *Melithaea* species. Photo by Walt Deas.

Closeup of the Magenta Sea Fan, *Melithaea* species. Photo by Walt Deas.

Melithaea species are so attractive that many beginners are tempted to buy them. RESIST THE TEMPTATION. To grow a Hammered Sea Fan like this one requires great skill and lots of luck. The luck comes in when the sea fan was collected and how much abuse it took. If they are carefully removed from their birthplace, they have a fair chance of surviving in the mini-reef aquarium providing they get back lighting as well as top lighting and gentle but thorough water movement. Photo by MP&C Piednoir Aqua Press.

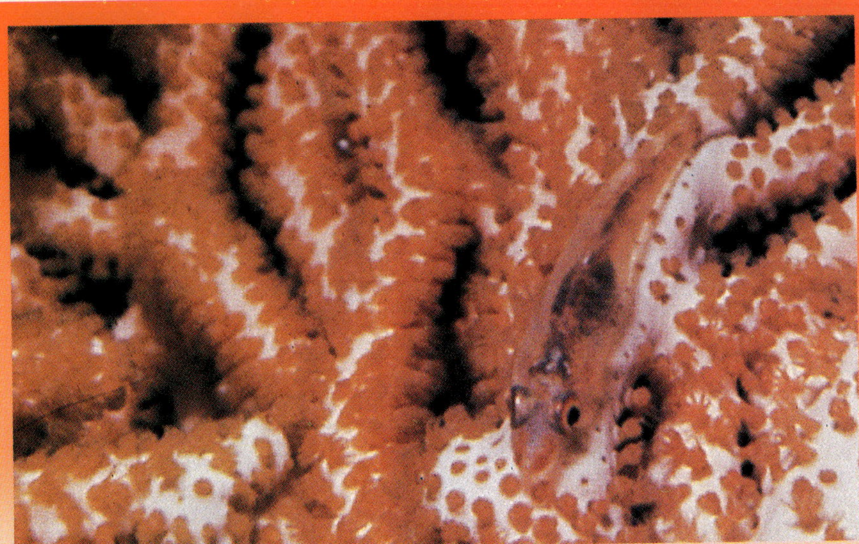

An unknown transparent Goby on this *Subergorgia* species. The gobies and other living things seem to keep the sea fans clean. Photo by Walt Deas.

Brown Mushroom Coral, *Actinodiscus* species, is easily maintained in the aquarium with 5 hours of intense lighting per day, slow water movements and isolation from other flower animals. Photo by Dr. Herbert R. Axelrod.

GREEN-RINGED ANEMONE CORAL, *Actinodiscus* species, is easily maintained in the mini-reef aquarium with 5 hours of intense lighting, slow-moving waters and isolation. These can be planted on the bottom of the tank where the light is lowest and the water is most placid. Photo by U. Erich Friese.

BROWN GIANT CUP, *Amplexidiscus* species, is relatively safe in the mini-reef aquarium with 5 hours of light, slow water movement and room to expand. Photo by MP&C Piednoir Aqua Press.

GOLDEN GIANT MUSHROOM CORAL, *Amplexidiscus* species, eating a mussel! Photo by MP&C Piednoir Aqua Press.

GOLDEN GIANT MUSHROOM CORAL, *Amplexidiscus* species, swallowing the mussel by closing itself over the shellfish. Photo by MP&C Piednoir Aqua Press.

BLUE GIANT MUSHROOM *Actinodiscus* species, has a smooth surface. Photo by U.Erich Friese.

PIMPLED BROWN MUSHROOM, *Actinodiscus* species has pimples. Photo by U.Erich Friese.

GIANT GREEN MUSHROOM, *Actinodiscus* species expanded, a sight you don't often see. It is easily cared for in the mini-reeftank. Photo by U. Erich Friese.

FALSE CORAL, *Rhodactis* species. Photo by R. Wederich.

BROWN MUSHROOM, *Actinodiscus* species, is easily maintained in the aquarium with 5 hours of intense lighting and slow water movements. Keep it from touching other flower animals. Photo by U. Erich Friese.

Actinodiscus species are wonderful in the mini-reef tank. They have a wide range of light tolerances so they can be planted at different levels in the tank (=different quantity and quality of light energy). They do best low in the tank where the water is not too active. Photo by MP&C Piednoir Aqua Press.

MOTTLED MUSHROOMS, *Actinodiscus* species, lived for 13 years in the author's tank. They reproduced freely. Photo by Dr. Herbert R. Axelrod.

BLUE MUSHROOM CORAL, *Actinodiscus coeruleus*, is attractive and easily cared for in the mini-reef tank. Photo by MP&C Piednoir Aqua Press.

Actinodiscus species require minimal light and slow water motion. They are called many things in the aquarium world such as Coral Anemones, False Corals, Mushroom Anemones and Disk Anemones. If you call them Mushrooms your dealer will know what you mean. Photo by Dr. Herbert R. Axelrod.

COMMON MUSHROOM CORAL, *Actinodiscus* species, is a welcome addition to every mini-reef tank. You don't see many mini-reefers that don't include this genus in their collection. Photo by MP&C Piednoir

***Actinodiscus* species.**

INDEX

Page numbers in **boldface** refer to illustrations.